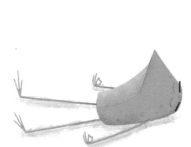

YOGA FROG

BY NORA CARPENTER

ILLUSTRATED BY MARK CHAMBERS

RP | KIDS
PHILADELPHIA

TO GAREK AND ZANDER,
MY OWN LITTLE YOGA FROGS.
–N.C.

FOR ELIZABETH, SOPHIE, ADAM, ELLIE, ALICE, AND
ALL THE OTHER YOGA FROGS AROUND THE WORLD!
–M.C.

Running Press Kids
Hachette Book Group
1290 Avenue of the Americas, New York, NY 10104
www.runningpress.com/rpkids
@RP_Kids

Printed in China

First Edition: May 2018

Published by Running Press Kids, an imprint of Perseus Books, LLC, a subsidiary of Hachette Book Group, Inc. The Running Press Kids name and log is a trademark of the Hachette Book Group.

The Hachette Speakers Bureau provides a wide range of authors for speaking events. To find out more, go to www.hachettespeakersbureau.com or call (866) 376-6591. The publisher is not responsible for websites (or their content) that are not owned by the publisher.

Print book cover and interior design by Frances J. Soo Ping Chow

Library of Congress Control Number: 2017951769

ISBNs: 978-0-7624-6467-8 (hardcover),
978-0-7624-6468-5 (ebook), 978-0-7624-9217-6 (ebook),
978-0-7624-9218-3 (ebook)

1010

10 9 8 7 6 5 4 3 2 1

Every morning Yoga Frog wakes with the sun and stretches his arms high above his head. Sometimes he's still tired. Sometimes he's even a tad grumpy. He isn't really a morning frog.

When he's not feeling his happy, froggy self, or if he wants to feel *better*, Yoga Frog knows just what to do: yoga! Join him!

MOUNTAIN

(TADASANA)

Stand straight and tall.

Imagine you are a mountain,
tough and unshakeable.

Take deep breaths,
feeling your body fill
with energy.

CHAIR

(UTKATASANA)

Sit in an
imaginary chair.

Lift your arms in front
or alongside your ears.

Feel your strength.

STAR

(UTTHITA TADASANA)

Standing, give yourself
a big hug, then *BAM*—

fling your arms wide and
jump your feet apart.

You're a star sending light
to the universe.

CRESCENT MOON

(ASHTA CHANDRASANA)

Stand with your feet touching
and arms up.

As you breathe out, bend into
a shining crescent moon.

Bend to your other side, then
return to Mountain.

TREE

(VRKSANANA)

Gazing at a spot ahead of you,
bring one foot to the opposite leg
(not on the knee).

Raise your arms skyward like
branches, breathing as you wobble.

Switch feet.

Tree Pose reminds us to embrace
flexibility and not be too stiff.

GIRAFFE
(VIRABHADRASANA I)

Step one foot forward,
bending the front knee slightly.

Clasp your hands above your head,
and stretch your whole body
as you reach high to the clouds.

After three breaths,
switch sides.

HAWK IN NEST

(BALASANA)

Flapping your wings,
fly down to your nest.

Tuck your legs beneath you as
you spread your wings over your
nest and take five slow breaths.

Resting helps your brain and
body stay strong.

COW

(BITILASANA)

Start on your hands and knees.

Tilt your chin up as you breathe in,

then arch your back and
tip your chin to your chest as
you breathe out into

CAT

(MARJARYASANA).

Repeat.

Your Cat-Cow flow keeps your
spine healthy and flexible.

DOWNWARD-FACING DOG

(ADHO MUKHA SVANASANA)

With your feet and hands
on the ground, lift your hips and
look between your knees.

Wag your tail! Bark!

If you are feeling extra playful,
you can kick your legs up, too.

WOLF

(VIRASANA)

Sit tall on your heels,
palms resting on your thighs.

You are a brave wolf keeping guard.

As you breathe, slowly turn
your head from side to side.

TURTLE
(SASANGASANA, MODIFIED)

Sit cross-legged.

Breathe out, and curl into your
safe, warm shell.

Take two deep breaths,
then sit up.

VOLCANO

(MALASANA)

Begin in a squat position.

Count down with Yoga Frog,
then erupt into the air.

3-2-1 KABOOM!

Repeat.

CATERPILLAR

(ARDHA MATSYENDRASANA)

Breathe in, and lift both arms.
Searching for a leaf to munch,
twist to the side.

Bring one hand to the floor behind
you and one to your thigh.

Breathe in and untwist.

Breathe out, and switch sides.

Breathe in back to center.

BUTTERFLY
(BADDHA KONASANA)

Place the soles of your feet together.

Gently flap your knees and wings as you flutter in the sky.

FISH

(MATSYASANA, MODIFIED)

Place your hands behind you while extending your legs like a fish tail.

Splash your friends.

BRIDGE

(SETU BANDHA SARVANGASANA)

Lying down, place the soles
of your feet on the floor.

Lift your hips.

After two breaths, slowly lower
your body down.

HAPPY BABY
(ANANDA BALASANA)

Lying on your back,
grab your feet and giggle.

Gently rock side to side.

RESTING POSE
(SAVASANA)

Close your eyes and rest
comfortably on the floor.

Listen to your breath roll in and out.

In. And out.

Smile.

Gently, sit up.

Thanks for helping Yoga Frog
return to his happy, hoppy self!

It's time for a great day.

A NOTE FOR PARENTS

The word *yoga* originates from the Sanskrit root *yuj*, meaning to join or unite. Therefore, a basic, child friendly definition of yoga is the union of body, breath, and mind. Kids don't need to intellectually understand this concept, though, to experience yoga's benefits. I've taught children as young as two who begin a session jittery and distracted, but then end up breathing peacefully in Balasana or Savasana. They don't consciously realize the yoga flow has calmed their bodies, which in turn has allowed them better focus. They just know yoga is fun and feels good.

Research shows the tremendous benefits yoga practices offer children: boosted confidence, increased self-control, increased sense of self-worth, increased fine and gross motor skills, decreased stress, better listening skills, et cetera. What's more, it is appropriate for any age/ability/special need. Listen to your body. If something doesn't feel good, adjust until it does or try a new pose.

The world can be a dizzying, stressful place for all ages, and the youngest among us often don't know how to handle that anxiety. They haven't learned (nor have many adults, for that matter!) that we regularly need a break from the go, go, go of life—a time to center and recharge. My hope is this book offers children (and their adult readers) a fun, accessible entry to the healing world of yoga.

The Poses (Asanas) and the Breath

Yoga Frog presents poses in a true yoga flow, with the earlier poses warming up muscles for the later poses, and the final poses cooling them down.

Sometimes people new to yoga accidentally hold their breath during the poses. That makes everything harder! Breathing slowly and evenly through the nose calms the nervous system. Additionally, listening to our breath gives our minds something to focus on so we're not thinking about our daily worries.

Namaste, and have fun!

—Nora Carpenter, Certified Yoga Teacher